The
Fabled Life
of Aesop

The Fabled Life of Aesop

by
Ian Lendler

illustrated by
Pamela Zagarenski

HOUGHTON MIFFLIN HARCOURT
Boston New York

One day, a slave was born.

It was sometime around 2,500 years ago and somewhere near Greece. No one knows for sure because the baby's parents were slaves too. No one recorded the history of slaves, so no one knows their names.

The only thing we know is the name they gave their baby boy . . .

"Aesop."

Aesop was taken from his parents and sent to work in the grape fields of Samos, a hot, dry island in the Mediterranean Sea.

Growing up, Aesop learned to speak differently from people who were free.

Slaves had to be careful what they said.

One day, out in the field, a slave said to Aesop, "I heard the master has smelly feet."

But the master overheard.

That person was never seen again.

So slaves learned to tell stories in ways that wouldn't get them in trouble. They spoke about the animals and the natural world around them.

The next day in the field, the person working next to Aesop said, "Did you hear the story about the lion? He stepped on a thorn and his paw got infected."

"Oh!" said Aesop. "So *that's* why his paw smells!"

Aesop learned to speak in code.

Everyone soon noticed there was something special about Aesop.

One day the water in the well dropped so low that the bucket couldn't reach. No one knew what to do.

But Aesop had an idea.

Everyone thought it was so clever that they all pitched in to help. The water began to rise, and when it reached the top, their cheers drew the attention of his master, Xanthus.

Xanthus decided to test Aesop.

He said, "You're clever enough to help slaves, but are you clever enough to help me?"

Aesop hesitated. He was scared.

He had to find a way to tell the truth without angering his master. He had to speak in code.

Aesop said . . .

One day, a mouse accidentally stepped on a sleeping lion. The lion woke and grabbed the mouse.

"Let me go!" begged the mouse. "Someday I'll repay you."

The lion laughed at the idea of a puny mouse helping him. But he let the mouse go.

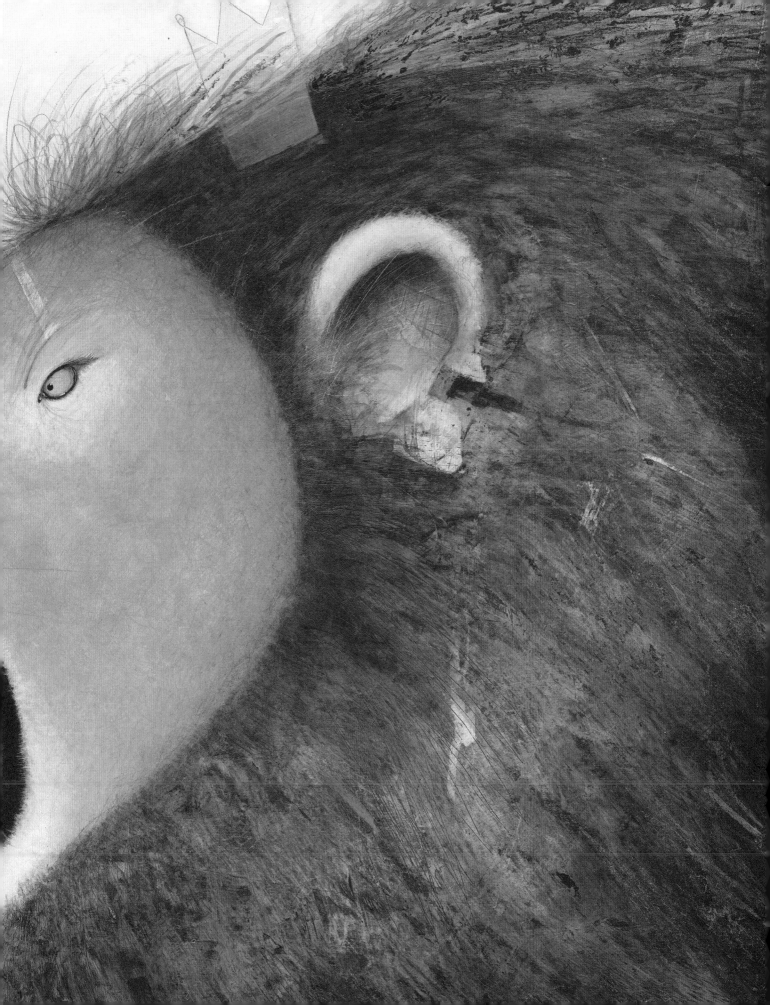

The next day, the lion got trapped in a
hunter's net. He roared helplessly.

The mouse came running. He gnawed at
the net until it broke. The lion was free!

"You see?" said the mouse. "Even a mouse
can help a mighty lion."

When Aesop finished his story, Xanthus laughed and said, "Very clever, indeed. Come work in my house, little mouse. You can chew on any nets that trap me."

Xanthus put Aesop to work running his business.

One day, Xanthus and another master named Jadon had an argument over money. To settle it, they summoned Aesop and ordered him to judge who was right.

Again, Aesop hesitated.

Whichever master he chose, the other would be angry. Either one could have him killed. He had to keep both masters happy.

He thought and thought and then he said . . .

One very hot day, a lion and a boar found a small watering hole.
They argued over who should drink first. They began to fight . . .

As they fought, they noticed that vultures were gathering,
waiting to eat the body of the loser.

The lion and the boar stopped fighting immediately and
shared the water. The vultures went hungry that day.

"So it's better to make peace with your friends," said Jadon, "than be eaten by your enemies."

The two masters agreed that Aesop's advice was very wise. They settled their argument peacefully.

Jadon was so impressed that he asked to buy Aesop. You see, no matter how clever or kind Aesop was, he was still just a slave and slaves were something to be bought and sold.

Xanthus agreed, and once again Aesop was taken away.

In his new home, Aesop went to work.

For every problem his new master faced, Aesop created a story about sly foxes, foolish farmers, or clever mice. The stories warned against greed and deceit. They taught the value of working hard and being honest, humble, and kind.

Many of them taught another hidden lesson as well. It was something no master would pick up on, but every slave or powerless person would understand. They taught them how to survive in a world that was sometimes unjust and cruel.

ÆSOP'S FABLES

The Tortoise and the Hare

Once a hare was making fun of a tortoise for being slow. "It's true, I am slow," said the tortoise, "but I can still beat you in a race."

The hare thought this was so funny that he agreed to the contest. All the animals in the forest gathered to watch.

As soon as the race started, the hare shot out of sight. At the halfway point, he was so far ahead that he decided to lie down and take a nap. Meanwhile, the tortoise kept walking, slowly and steadily, never stopping.

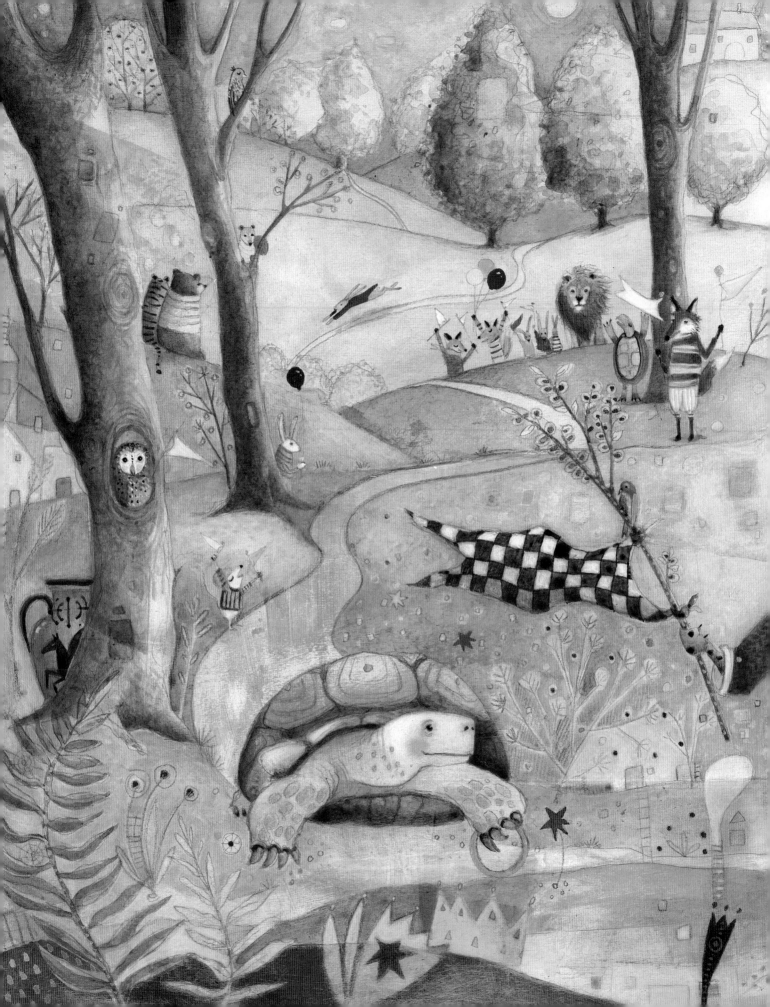

After a while, he passed the napping hare and headed toward the finish line. The animals began to cheer on the tortoise. Their cheers woke the hare, who saw the tortoise far ahead. The hare sprinted toward the finish line, but he was too late. The tortoise had won!

Slow and steady wins the race.

The Boy Who Cried Wolf

A shepherd boy was tending his sheep in a field near a dark forest. It was boring work so he decided to have some fun. He rushed into his village shouting, "WOLF! WOLF!"

The villagers ran out to the field with pitchforks. But when the shepherd boy started laughing, the villagers realized they'd been tricked. They shook their heads and went home.

The next day, the shepherd boy did it again. "WOLF! WOLF!" he cried even louder. Again, the villagers ran out to help him. Again, they realized they'd been tricked and walked home, grumbling.

The third day, the shepherd boy saw an actual wolf come out of the dark forest. "WOLF! WOLF!" he cried in panic. But this time, no one came to help. So the wolf ate the entire flock, and then, for dessert, he ate the shepherd boy too.

No one believes a liar, even when they tell the truth.

The North Wind and the Sun

The north wind and the sun were trying to decide who was more powerful. When they saw a traveler walking down the road, the sun said, "Let's have a contest. Whoever can remove that man's coat is the strongest."

"That's easy," said the north wind, and he began to blow. He tore at the man's coat with powerful, icy blasts. But the traveler only wrapped his coat tighter around himself.

The north wind gave up, exhausted. "It's impossible," he said.

Then it was the sun's turn. She began to shine. The air turned lovely and warm. The traveler unbuttoned his coat. Soon, the traveler decided to enjoy the sunny day, so he lay down in the shade of a tree and took off his coat.

People respond better to kindness than to force.

The Fox and the Grapes

A hungry fox came across a bunch of ripe, juicy grapes growing high above his head. The fox's mouth began to water, so he jumped up to grab them. He missed.

So he took a running jump . . . and missed again. The fox jumped and jumped, but he could not reach the grapes.

Finally, he looked at the grapes scornfully and said, "That's okay. I didn't actually want those grapes. They're probably sour."

Then, he turned and walked away with contempt.

It is easy to pretend to dislike what you cannot have.

The Donkey and the Lapdog

There once was a farmer who owned a donkey and a lapdog.

The farmer treated the donkey well. He gave him a nice stable, fresh hay, and plenty of water. But in exchange, the donkey had to work in the field all day long.

Meanwhile, the donkey saw the lapdog living in the farmer's house and eating scraps from his table. The lapdog's only job was to lie in the farmer's lap and wag his tail. The donkey became jealous.

"Perhaps if I act like the dog," the donkey thought, "the master will start loving me the same way."

The next day, the donkey escaped his harness and ran into the kitchen where the farmer was eating his lunch. The donkey wagged his tail furiously like the lapdog, breaking all the dishes on the table.

Then the donkey jumped into the farmer's lap . . . and knocked him onto the floor. The farmer yelled for help and the farmhands rushed in and dragged the donkey away.

Don't try to make others like you by being something that you're not.

The Goose and the Golden Egg

There was once a poor farmer who was amazed to discover that one of his geese laid a golden egg.

Every day, that goose laid a single golden egg. The farmer and his wife were soon quite rich. But it wasn't long before they became unhappy. They weren't getting rich fast enough. So they decided to kill the goose and take all the gold at once.

But when they opened the goose up, there was nothing inside. Their goose was dead, and they never got another golden egg again.

If you always want more, you'll lose what you have.

The Fox and the Crow

One bright morning, a fox spotted a crow high up in a nearby tree with a hunk of cheese in her mouth.

The fox approached the foot of the tree and called up, "My, what a beautiful creature you are!"

The crow looked down at the fox suspiciously and said nothing.

The fox continued to flatter the crow, "I've never seen a creature as perfect as you! Your wings are splendid, and your feathers positively gleam in the sun! I only wish I could hear your voice. If it's half as beautiful as the rest of you, I would declare you the queen of all birds!"

The crow was so pleased by the fox's compliments that she forgot her suspicions. She opened her mouth to caw . . . and down fell the cheese—straight into the fox's mouth!

"Thank you," said the fox with a grin. "In exchange for the snack, I will give you a piece of advice . . .

"Never trust a flatterer."

The Town Mouse and the Country Mouse

A town mouse once went to visit her cousin out in the country. The country mouse served her seeds, roots, and acorns and cold creek water to drink. That night, they went to sleep under a bush.

The next day, the town mouse said to her cousin, "You cannot possibly be happy living like this. Come to the city and you will see how much better life can be."

So the country mouse followed her cousin to a large house in the city. They entered the dining room and saw the remnants of the owner's feast. The country mouse couldn't believe her eyes—there was cheese and meat and fruit and sweets. But just as she was about to take a bite, she heard a growling noise.

"Uh-oh," said the town mouse.

Massive dogs burst through the door. The two mice ran underneath a teacup just in time. They hid there, trembling and scared, until the dogs went away. Then the town mouse said, "We can go back out to eat. I think the coast is clear."

But when she looked over, she saw that the country mouse had packed her bags and put on her coat. "Goodbye, Cousin," said the country mouse.

It is better to live a simple life in peace than a luxurious life filled with fear.

The Ant and the Grasshopper

One warm summer's day, a grasshopper was merrily chirping and making music when he saw an ant walk by. The ant was struggling to carry a kernel of corn back to his nest.

The grasshopper called to the ant, "Why are you working so hard? Come sing with me!"

"I'm storing food for winter," said the ant. "You should do the same."

"Winter? Who cares about winter?" said the grasshopper. "There's plenty of food today."

The ant continued with his work. The grasshopper continued to play. Then, winter came. The grasshopper couldn't find food, and he had nothing saved. He was starving, so he begged the ant for a bite to eat.

The ant told the grasshopper, "Since you spent all summer singing, you can dance to bed without supper."

There's a time for work and a time for play.

The Lion and the Statue

One day, a man and a lion were arguing over who was more powerful. The man claimed humans were more powerful because of their intelligence. To prove his point, the man pointed to a nearby statue of a man defeating a lion in combat.

The lion just laughed. "That only proves that a man made that statue. If I made a statue, the lion would be the victor."

There's more than one side to every story, and the moral depends on who tells it.

With the help of Aesop's stories, Jadon became a successful and well-respected man, not just in business, but in life. He became a wiser and more generous person. He learned to treat others with respect.

One day, he said to Aesop, "I would like to reward you for your service. Ask me for anything, Aesop, and I will grant your wish."

This time, Aesop did not hesitate.

He told a story he'd probably wanted to tell his entire life.

One day, a wolf was weak with hunger . . .

A house-dog saw the wolf and said, "Cousin, you'll die in the wild. Come work for my master. He'll feed you every day."

The wolf was so hungry he agreed and followed the dog home.

As they walked, the wolf noticed the fur on the dog's neck was worn away.

"Oh, that's nothing," said the dog. "That's where my master chains me. You get used to it."

"In that case," said the wolf, "goodbye, Cousin. I would rather starve while I'm free than be well fed in chains."

When Aesop finished speaking, Jadon fell silent. He thought for a long time. And then . . .

Æsop

The Ant and the Dove ∞ The grateful heart will always find opportunity∞

The Bear and the Bees ∞ The Lion and the Mouse ∞ The Tortoise and the Hare ∞ The Fox and the Grapes∞

Don't count your chickens before they're hatched. ∞ Slow and steady wins the race. ∞ You make more friends∞ There's strength in numbers∞ 12345678910 ∞

No act of kindness, no matter how small, is ever wasted. ∞ Gratitude is the s

Beware that you do not lose the substance by grasping at the shadow. ∞ Beauty is only skin-d

Birds of a feather flock together. ∞ It is not only fine feathers that make fine birds

∞ now its gratitude. ∞ Look before you leap. ∞ Jupiter and the birds.

The Dog in the Manger ∞ The Wolf in Sheep's Clothing

and the Pitcher ∞ The Dog in the Manger

than with force. ∞ A bird in hand is worth two in the bush. ∞

noble souls. ∞ There's a time for work and a time for play.

is the mother of invention. ∞ Be careful of the company you keep.

. . . he granted Aesop's wish.

For the first time in his life, Aesop was free.

53

Soon, everyone had heard about the slave who was so wise that he had been set free. They went to him for help and advice.

Aesop's stories were so memorable that they were told and retold in the streets.

As the years went by, the masters grew old and passed away. Their wealth and lands were lost. Their names were forgotten.

Aesop, too, eventually passed away. But his fame kept growing.

His stories were repeated in homes and town squares for generations. For centuries . . .

. . . until one day someone gathered them together in a book and called them

Aesop's Fables.

It became one of the most popular books in history.

THE BEASTS of the field

BEAR

King

T

THE ANT GRASSHOPPER love sheep BOY cup.

PEACOCK
butterfly
CHICKENS AND EGGS
watched a flock of sheep

A HARE one day ridiculed the short feet and slow pace of the Tortoise. The latter, laughing, said: "Though you be swift as the wind, I will beat you in a race."

suns and moons

clever FOX
THE WOLF IN SHEEP'S CLOTHING
THE CRANE

Golden Eggs
Lion in Love
The grateful heart
"My name is Truth,"

GOOSE
tortoise
Dog
WOLF
PEACE Frog

Fox having
THE FAMISHED
A Lion was aw
truth.

And in its pages, Aesop—the boy who was born a slave, who told stories to escape—traveled further than any king and lived longer than any empire.

He traveled across languages, countries, and continents.

He traveled across 2,500 years of time to be here today.

And now that you've heard his stories, he can travel for a while with you.

The End

Afterword

Fable is more historical than fact, because fact tells us about one man and fable tells us about a million men.
—Gilbert K. Chesterton, writer/philosopher

You are holding in your hands some of the oldest stories in human existence. Fables—loosely defined as stories with talking animals that teach a lesson—have been found on stone tablets dating back to 1500 BCE in Sumeria (modern-day Iraq).

However, fables became truly popular around 700 BCE in ancient Greece. They were a part of everyday life, used by politicians, poets, and anyone else who wanted to prove a point. Through frequent retellings in this era, old fables were sharpened and refined. New ones were invented. Fables became an art form.

Despite the widespread use of fables, the name that became most associated with them was Aesop. The name and the story of Aesop's life became well known in ancient Greece, and for good reason. The story becomes even more extraordinary *after* he was freed.

By that time, Aesop was so renowned for his ability to persuade others that people paid him to argue their cases in court. King Croesus, the famously wealthy local ruler, soon heard about Aesop and hired him as an advisor. Thus, Aesop became the trusted right-hand man to the richest king in history!

Aesop's story is so unbelievable that it's worth asking . . . is it true?

The answer is, we just don't know.

Historical records from that time are very limited, and records of individual slaves are nonexistent. Thus, there is no record of a date or place of birth for Aesop. There is no statue or image of what Aesop looked like. And since fables began as an oral tradition, there is no evidence of someone named Aesop personally writing down his stories.

To some historians, this suggests that Aesop was more like Mother Goose, a fictional figure created as a vehicle for all fable-like stories. On the other hand, Aesop's name *does* appear several times in historical records (starting approximately one hundred years after his supposed death), where he is referred to as "a fellow slave . . . the story writer."

In many ways, it doesn't matter if Aesop the person was real or not, because as the quote above shows, the *story* of Aesop's life—the story retold in this book—was common knowledge at that time. This tells us a lot about the culture that gave birth to many of our most famous fables.

Ancient Greece is commonly referred to as the cradle of Western civilization. It was also the birthplace of democracy, theater, and modern philosophy, along with fables. However, it was entirely built through slavery. Approximately one-quarter of the population of ancient Greece were slaves. Slaves were used on farms, in houses, even as shopkeepers and civil servants. In this atmosphere, in which a great civilization and great suffering were intertwined, is it any wonder that the story of a slave who uses his wits to win his freedom (and great success) would be appealing?

Against this background, we can see that even though "Aesop's Fables" are now interpreted as simple lessons on virtue and good values, many of them are actually practical advice on how to survive in a world in which some have power and some do not.

This life story was passed along orally for hundreds of years until the first century BCE, when it was formally written down (along with some of the fables themselves) in a book called *The Life of Aesop*. Historians call *The Life of Aesop* "one of the few genuinely popular books that have come down to us from ancient times."

It is also the very first book in history told from the point of view of a slave.

Aesop's life story was "popular." It was a story told not by kings or priests or those in power, but by common people. Because of this, it remained widely known for the next 1,500 years. So much so that when the printing press was invented in the fifteenth century, the first book printed was the Bible and the first illustrated book was *The Life of Aesop*!

Since then, the fables created during Aesop's time have proved to be the most durable stories in human history. Over the centuries, they have been translated into hundreds of languages. As they spread around the globe, countries and cultures of every type saw them as the perfect stories to explain their values. Their morals ("slow and steady wins the race," "don't count your chickens before they're hatched") have become part of humankind's communal wisdom.

That is the key to the popularity of "Aesop's Fables." They do not tell the story of one person or one people. They tell the story of *all* people.

They are the simplest form of storytelling, yet they help guide us through the most difficult journey that any of us face—making our way through life.

Bibliography

Bader, Barbara. *Aesop & Company.* Boston: Houghton Mifflin Company, 1991.

Lenaghan, R. T., ed. *Caxton's Aesop.* Cambridge, MA: Harvard University Press, 1967.

Library of Congress. "Aesop for Children." read.gov/aesop/index.html.

McKendry, John J., ed. *Aesop: Five Centuries of Illustrated Fables.* New York: The Metropolitan Museum of Art, 1964.

Patterson, Annabel. *Fables of Power: Aesopian Writing and Political History.* Durham, NC: Duke University Press, 1991.

Simondi, Tom. "Fables of Aesop." fablesofaesop.com.

Temple, Olivia, and Robert Temple, eds. *The Complete Fables.* New York: Penguin Classics, 1998

Zipes, Jack, ed. *Aesop's Fables.* New York: Signet Classics, 1992.

To my dad, the best unpaid research
assistant in the world —I. L.

For my family and especially Luka, I love you.
For Ann, my incredible editor, thank you.
*"The grateful heart will always find opportunities
to show its gratitude."* ~Aesop
—P. Z.

The fables in this book were illustrated with acrylics painted on wood panels. To show contrast, the illustrations
for the biography section were created in watercolors on watercolor paper with minor mixed media collage.
The text type was set in Andrade Pro.
The display type was set in Esmeralda Pro.

Designed by Whitney Leader-Picone

Library of Congress Cataloging-in-Publication Data
Names: Lendler, Ian, author. | Zagarenski, Pamela, illustrator.
Title: The fabled life of Aesop / by Ian Lendler ; illustrated by Pamela
Zagarenski.
Other titles: Aesop's fables.
Description: Boston : Houghton Mifflin Harcourt, [2020].
Identifiers: LCCN 2018052167 | ISBN 9781328585523 (hardcover picture book)
Subjects: LCSH: Aesop—Juvenile literature. | Authors, Greek—Biography—Juvenile
literature. | Aesop's fables—Juvenile literature.
Classification: LCC PA3851.A2 L46 2020 | DDC 398.24/52—dc23
LC record available at https://lccn.loc.gov/2018052167

Manufactured in China
SCP 10 9 8 7 6 5 4 3 2 1
4500785150